EIGHT
STEPS TO
INTIMACY

EIGHT STEPS TO INTIMACY

JOHN TRENT, Ph.D.

MOODY PRESS
CHICAGO

© 1994 by
JOHN TRENT, PH.D.

All Scripture quotations are taken from the *New American Standard Bible,* © 1960, 1962, 1963, 1968, 1971, 1972, 1973, 1975, and 1977 by The Lockman Foundation, and are used by permission.

ISBN: 0-8024-3713-3

7 9 10 8 6

Printed in the United States of America

At age thirty-one, Jim remained in high school shape. Intelligent and energetic, he was indispensable at work. He also was incredibly lonely at home.

After playing the dating game since college without success, Jim finally found the one woman in an oceanful of choices who washed away all his defenses. With just a smile, Becky could warm his heart and cause chills to come over him at the same time. And while he thought he'd been inoculated against falling in love, this time he was sure he'd caught the real thing. Then came the problem.

After years of waiting and watching, how could he really know if this was God's person for him? How could he be certain that this was genuine love? Or was this just an emotional state that would slip away like it did in so many other relationships?

Can someone really know if he is in love—the kind of love that God honors and that could point to a healthy, fulfilling future? Jim wondered.

Brian was forty-three. Slightly overweight, he struggled at times to keep up with yard work and a demanding job. And he sagged behind in being the father and husband he knew he should be.

His marriage with Shirley had started off fine. But somewhere between three corporate moves and two children, they'd lost the flame. In fact, it was now painfully obvious to both of them that the love they had for each other was barely a spark. *Were it not for our children, and our thin attachment to our church. . . .* Brian shuddered to think that he could even dream of tossing in the towel and leaving home—but that's exactly what he'd been thinking.

What is real love? Brian asked himself.

What was it that he and Shirley had walked away from, without even realizing they'd made a wrong turn? What could he do to pull his family together? To rekindle a flame that he knew God wanted for them? To build the kind of love that would have him and Shirley standing together, hand in hand and heart to heart? He wanted to hold Shirley's hand—at his fiftieth high school reunion and beyond.

As you read this booklet, you may be like Jim or Brian. While the differences between them were striking, they both suffered from the same thing: *Each man needed to understand in his world what genuine love looked like.* They needed to capture true love's reflection and display its colors like light through a prism.

Perhaps you're single, looking for some kind of clarity about your dating relationships. Wanting to build a foundation that is crisscrossed with reinforced concrete, not the sinking sand you see in so many friends' marriages. *You can.* God gives us a clear picture of what a godly courtship should look like. He provides us with a biblical blueprint for understanding if we're really in love—and if our courtship is laying sound pillars for a fulfilling future.

You may be married. Wanting to not just endure being married, but to experience the kind of closeness you know deep inside is possible. To look into her eyes and see them light up when you meet after work. To have her respond to your touch without pulling away. To have her verbally appreciate your efforts at the job and around the house. And to know deep inside that she's proud that of all the choices she could have made, you're the husband she'd pick all over again.

Fantasy? No. It can happen. It *should* happen. The same eight principles that God gives in a single chapter of the Bible can revolutionize a courtship or equip you as a married man to build an intimate relationship. Despite the difficulties you may have had in the past, you can begin to build your love around God's unchangeable Word today and see positive, God-honoring results.

All this from one chapter of the Bible?

That's right. Because in an often overlooked book of the Old Testament, God has hidden riches for those who'll search. Eight relational gems that we'll mine together in this booklet, and that can become an everyday part of your life.

The Greatest Love Story Ever Written

What would you say is the greatest love story of all time? Would it be the classic play *Romeo and Juliet*? A novel such as *A Tale of Two Cities* or *Les Miserables*? Perhaps it's a true romance, such as Grace Kelly marrying the Prince of Monaco. You may recall an old movie, such as *Gone with the Wind* or *Love Story*.

While the world may argue over what the greatest love story is, the Creator of romance has already titled it. It's called the "Song of Solomon."

In chapter 1, verse 1, we read the credits, which call the book "The Song of Songs, which is Solomon's." In the Old Testament, if you wanted to say something was tremendous, incredible, without equal or rival, (or "rad!" as today's teens say), you'd repeat the attribute. For example, in the book of Isaiah, the Lord is presented as the "King of Kings" and the "Lord of Lords." In other words, He is the Almighty King above all kings, and the very Lord of all.

Thus, as this book begins we learn that this is the "Song of Songs." The greatest love story ever written—and it's one that can teach us much about fulfilling pre-marital and marital love. Chapter 1 contains eight steps to a lasting, genuine love. They build intimacy in marriage.

The Foundations and Steps

"Whooooooooaaaa, right there!" you may be thinking. "You may have your Ph.D., Trent, but any fool can tell you that Solomon can't be the greatest example of love. After all, wasn't he the same guy who had dozens of wives and hundreds of concubines? What's real love got to do with him?"

Actually, plenty. Toward the later part of his life, King Solomon did begin to take foreign wives and concubines—adding up to the hundreds. Yet when did that practice begin? In the Scriptures, you'll read that it was *after* a visit by the Queen of Sheba that Solomon began to walk away from God's best, and to practice what was common in other neighboring cultures, namely, multiplying wives and concubines.

In Solomon's earlier years—when he was content with asking for wisdom and guidance from God, rather than adding wives or seeking after pleasure—he was a man who walked the walk. He obeyed and pleased God. And therein lies a powerful lesson for any of us who take a serious look at biblical love.

Even if we're the wisest man on earth, if we start walking away from God's best, we start walking toward a cliff. If we're not centering our relationship squarely on God's Word, then we're building on a known fault line and are simply a disaster waiting to happen.

Solomon may have been a part of the greatest love story of all time—but he walked away from God's best. So to make sure that doesn't happen to you or me, let's move forward to look at these eight marks of lasting love. They are eight steps to intimacy.

We begin, though, with a firm foundation: we must know the Creator behind human love. We must walk with Him. That means having a relationship founded on Jesus Christ's reconciling us to God, giving us the desire to obey and please God.

A house of love begins with the foundation of knowing God and obeying Him.

That's the foundation. From there we climb the steps and enter the door to intimacy between a man and a woman. Each one of these eight steps is an aspect of caring that we have to practice each day and hold on to through each season of life.

The Steps to Intimacy

1. STRONG PHYSICAL ATTRACTION
   (CAREFUL PHYSICAL RESTRAINT)

All eight steps, based on Song of Songs, contribute to intimacy. We must emphasize that they also become marks of a genuine love; that is, these actions and attitudes demonstrate a developing love. The first way you can develop a God-honoring, genuine love in your relationship can be found in the words of Solomon's fiancée. In Song 1:2a, she reveals part of her thoughts during Solomon's courtship. "May he kiss me with the kisses of his mouth!"

That's a soon-to-be bride asking that her fiancé kiss her—and more than once! And though we may blush at the thought, God doesn't hesitate to record a clear picture that *strong physical desire* is a part of a healthy courtship. However, before someone picks up stones and cries, "License!" it's important to realize that along with that desire must come strong physical restraint.

Although a strong attraction exists between them, it is not until their wedding night (recorded in Song 4) that the couple moves beyond theory to application of their desires. Yet the message is clear. For those wondering if they're really in love (or assessing the state of their love today), strong physical attraction is one aspect of genuine love. Its presence is one mark of true love, though by itself it can never sustain love.

Physical attraction is something that Mark and Ann both struggled with. They were in the same college group at their church, and over the years they watched many, many friends meet in the class and move toward marriage.

Mark was outgoing, liked by everyone, and set perhaps the single season record for being in friends's weddings with eight. Ann, on the other hand, watched as a steady parade of roommates and Bible study friends met, married, and moved out into the young marrieds' class and married student housing.

Theirs was a developing friendship—an important place to begin. Yet as the group thinned out by marriage, almost by default they kept being tossed together. Finally, they began dating and with the cheers (and strong-armed pushing) of their friends, moved into an uneasy courtship. They stayed together, yet both of them knew that, among other things, any kind of physical spark was missing.

In this age where sex is pictured as everything, the absence of physical attraction or temptation kept their focus on Christ and purity. Yet both of them struggled inside with a genuine disinterest toward each other —especially physically—that moved far beyond physical restraint.

Now, five years into marriage there is not only low sexual desire in their marriage, but no sexual involvement. And while, again, sex is overblown in our godless culture, their lack of attraction toward each other has contributed much to their present struggles.

During their second year of marriage, Mark began an addiction to pornography. Lately Ann has seen her sense of worth, value, and beauty plummet into a dark abyss.

I'm not suggesting that Mark's move toward pornography and Ann's lack of self-worth were the result of their not being attracted to each other. But the lack of any type of physical spark in courtship and beyond certainly did add to their problems. What's more, it robbed them of a powerful tool to protect their marital purity, and deprived them of a source of God-given emotional delight.

In 1 Corinthians 7:5, Paul specifically notes that a man and wife are not to deprive each other of intimacy except for a "time." That's for a specific reason, namely that sexual temptation lies right at the door if we withhold ourselves from each other for long periods. Sexual intimacy in marriage is not just an aid to facing temptation; it yields genuine enjoyment, a by-product of the act of marriage that God Himself designed. In Proverbs 5:19, we read that for the husband, it's his wife's breasts that should "satisfy [him] at all times." Later in the Song of Songs, at the end of a wedding night filled with intimacy, God Himself speaks and says of their union, "Eat, friends; drink and imbibe deeply, O lovers" (5:1b).

While it's not the most important aspect of a courtship or marriage by any means, the presence (or absence) of that God-given romantic spark is one way to assess the level of love in the relationship.

But what if you're a married man reading this booklet and you've seen your wife's physical desires steadily *decrease* over the years? I've met many a man who would love to hear the words from his wife, "May he kiss me with the kisses of his mouth!" However, their wives have little interest.

Where does that strong physical desire on the part of Solomon's bride (and women today as well) come from? It comes from the next important aspect of genuine, biblical love that many of us give more attention to in our courtship than when we are married. It too is a key to intimacy, another entry point into the house of love.

2. A PURIFIED CHARACTER

Why is she so desirous of kissing him? What sparks passion like that? Here in the Scriptures (and even in clinical studies today), it's not a man's biceps, boat, or even his bank account that keeps and maintains that strong desire. It's something far deeper . . . his character. Her passion is based on his character.

Listen as Solomon's bride tells us where that romantic spark sprung from:

> *May he kiss me with the kisses of*
> *his mouth!*
> *For your love is better than wine.*
> *Your oils have a pleasing*
> *fragrance,*
> *Your name is like purified oil.*
> (1:2–3)

Howard Hendricks, my friend and seminary professor emeritus, always pounded into our heads in class, "Men, when you see the word *for* or *therefore*, ask what they're there for!"

Here, the word *for* is there to show how Solomon's bride clearly links her passion level with what she sees on the inside, not the outside. Being around him is pleasant, like a pleasing fragrance (not musk!). And then she explains why: "Your name is like purified oil."

What she's saying here would have been crystal clear to Solomon or any reader of his day. In Old Testament thought, a person's name stood for far more than just something to put on a business card. It was representative of all that person was and who he could become. That's why God would sometimes change a person's name in the Scriptures (like Abram to Abraham, and later Simon to Peter).

And what did Solomon's name picture for her? The finest of "purified oil."

Unless you have traveled to the Holy Land, you probably haven't seen a demonstration of how they purified oil in Solomon's day. Let me explain to you one process that was commonly used.

After mashing the olives, the farmer would pour the unrefined oil and pulp through a series of trays, one stacked on top of the other, and each filled with decreasing sized rocks. Thus larger rocks would be at the top and filter out the biggest sediments, while each progressive layer of smaller stones and finally sand would allow for the pure, refined olive oil to collect in a scooped-out cistern (a holding area in a rock) beneath the trays.

In other words, as Solomon's bride pictures him, he is someone whose life has been filtered from impurities. In the way he carries himself, he's a man of manners and dignity. Not the kind of guy who would belch at the table for a laugh (even though belching in Solomon's day didn't carry the same crudeness). And even more, he's a man whose character reflects an inner integrity that promotes her passion.

James never recognized that missing element of character as a reason behind his wife's low sexual interest. When Diane and he came in for counseling, they were as tense as any couple I'd seen. And like many couples involved in ongoing conflict, they had a minimal sexual relationship. As we talked, guess what showed up as a core reason for her disinterest in her husband physically? It didn't have anything to do with his physique. It had everything to do with a character issue that he blew off as minor—and she looked at as major.

James ran a small business out of their home, and while he was out making calls, Diane would often be the one who answered the phone. Yet with cash flow a real problem, some of the callers became quite angry, demanding late payments.

When James was home, she'd often hear him lie to a vendor, going far beyond the simple, "The check's in the mail." And soon James would demand that she lie for him too when she answered the phone, all in an effort to buy more time to work out his business finances.

What James didn't realize was that buying time was also purchasing major problems in his marriage. The huge withdrawals he was making from his wife's emotional bank account by forcing her to lie for him—and watching him fabricate stories himself—resulted in a zero balance when he tried to draw any warmth or affection from his wife. Diane also lost a full level of respect for James, and this undercut any passionate feelings for her husband.

The average man doesn't realize how powerfully a woman's desire is sparked by a godly character. Cheat on our taxes . . . and watch her security level drop. Scream at the children . . . and forget intimacy that night.

Solomon certainly had a godly character during this time of his life, and his bride responded with unforced physical attention.

3. RESPECTED BY OTHERS

The third step toward a house of love actually is laid by others. Outsiders recognize and appreciate what the couple sees inside. As the groom's lover declares:

> *May he kiss me with the kisses of*
> *his mouth!*
> *For your love is better than wine.*
> *Your oils have a pleasing*
> *fragrance,*
> *Your name is like purified oil.*
> *Therefore the maidens love you.*

As we continue our look at the keys to intimacy, here's an element of genuine love that is also linked with the woman's appreciation for a man's character. Namely, the woman is not alone in seeing how valuable he is. Those friends and ladies of the court saw Solomon's life, and they too were deeply taken by the kind of man he was.

Why is this such a key element of biblical love? Because others often can recognize character, and we need their confirmation or warnings about a person's nature. Knowing this before marriage is especially helpful.

Many people I see in counseling have found that their "love" for another person came in the form of trying to "help" or "rescue" him or her—often against the advice of everyone else around them.

Angela, for example, was compassionate, caring, kind, and came from a loving Christian home. That's one reason why her friends and family were so concerned when a friendship with a young man who "walked on the wild side" turned into a dating relationship.

Angela just knew that she could change him. She could see so clearly the potential and warmth that were trapped deep inside. Yet other people saw only his anger and an attitude that spelled trouble both for Angela and anyone else he was around.

They did marry—and divorced within a year. And while no one actually said, "I told you so," Angela had ignored an important element of biblical love. Namely, like a "light set on a hill," others around us should be able to see and appreciate our loved one's character and lifestyle.

If you're the only one in a courtship who sees any value in the person you're dating (apart from her being created in God's image), watch out. No pilot would try to land a plane on a runway where flight crews were waving him off. There may be a good reason your parents are waving red warning flags instead of simply trying to "control" you. There may be more love than jealousy behind your friends telling you you're making a major mistake.

If one aspect of genuine love is physical attraction, and another is our character, a third important element is the appraisal of others on our loved one.

The important factor here if we're married is that winning the respect of those in our home first—and then of those outside—comes with a purified character. All of us, in some ways, could be considered "damaged goods." None of us is perfect. Each of us needs a Savior to deliver us and forgive us of our sins. But if you want to see genuine love bloom and flower over the marital life cycle, then a purified, godly character that is both loved by your spouse and appreciated by those outside is a key to keeping the flame alive day after day.

4. A BIBLICAL BALANCE IN OUR ROLES

We've seen three things in this greatest of all love stories that can point us toward lasting love: strong physical desire (with appropriate restraint during courtship); a purified life that your lover can value; and the respect of others, who can see high value in your loved one.

Add to these an important statement by Solomon's bride, and we have the fourth element of genuine love, one that can defeat the cultural confusion we face today.

In this age of "women's rights," "gay rights," and "animal rights," every group seems to be staking their claim to power—and setting off major power struggles as a result. The same thing is true in many homes. Power struggles often develop between spouses who are saying verbally or non verbally, "I'm in charge here!" Power struggles can escalate to all-out war and often result in both partners becoming casualties.

In contrast, biblical love gives us a clear picture of the best basis to build a marriage. A type of leadership model for the home that provides honoring decision making and welcomed marital roles. And we see that in the future bride's words and conclusion, "Draw me after you and let us run together!" (1:4)

In this clear picture of God's best for a marriage, we see two vivid indications of how a relationship should be structured. Reread this verse and then answer this question: Who is she asking to take the lead in their courtship and beyond?

Yes, it's Solomon. "Draw me after you" implies—actually states—her request that her husband take the lead. And while you might think I've heard just the opposite, if there is one cry I've heard from women in conferences across this nation, it's that very call for their husbands to lead.

For many of us men, we don't take the spiritual or emotional "lead" in our homes. Such an attitude of attention to work and passivity at work led to the best-selling book entitled, *Passive Men and Wild Women!*

Where does the absence of leadership come from in many homes? From many sources.[1] Partly because, like me, we've come from single-parent homes where we never saw a biblical model of godly leadership. (My father left our family when I was three months old, and I never met him until I was in my last years of high school.)

Second, many men have become so conditioned by the radical feminist agenda and liberal press that we think any type of male leadership is wrong. That's not true! When the Lord identified who was the "greatest" of all—the top of the top in terms of power and influence—guess who He pointed to. A servant. And as the leaders of our homes, that's a clear calling we men have: To become the leader in serving those God has given us.

It's not just because the Song of Songs is "ancient history" that this woman is desirous for Solomon to take the lead in their relationship. From Genesis 3 forward, there has been a God-designed hierarchy in the home and a desire for a woman to follow a godly man; and yet what many of us have confused as leadership is actually "lordship."

We are to have one God, one Lord. A man is not to "lord it over" those in his care, like power-hungry nonbelievers. Rather, as the head server in the family, he can find out what is needed in the home to build security, love, and strength with his wife and children—and then watch his wife be thrilled that he's taking that kind of lead! We men are not to be lords over our women. We are to be leaders to our women.

And just to clarify that it's leadership of a team that God has given us, listen to the rest of what Solomon's bride has to say: "Draw me after you [take the spiritual and emotional lead, men!], *and let us run together!*" (emphasis added)

Solomon's bride loves and asks for his leadership because she knows he's a man of godly character and warmth. What's more, while he's in the lead, she knows the journey they're on is a shared one.

Leadership that respects a spouse's feelings, desires, opinions, and convictions leads a wife (or fiancée) to ask us to lead on! It's not a demeaning subjugation, but an honoring linkage that moves both people toward the goal of greater love, and honoring God in the process.

Unfortunately, that's not the kind of love and leadership Larry demonstrated. Larry would demand his way on even the smallest thing with his wife. He demanded that the knife, fork, and spoon be laid out "just so," and he told his wife exactly when and how long she could be on the phone. Things became so bad in this out-of-control controller's home that he took to writing down the odometer reading in his wife's car. Each morning he'd log the mileage before going to work, and at night, he'd calculate "exactly were she'd been" and demand a report if the "miles" didn't add up.

That's not leadership; that's demeaning control—a strangling, self-absorbed rulership that resulted in his wife seeking a divorce.

High control people can miss God's best when it comes to a fulfilling, lasting relationship. Demanding controllers in a marriage can end up a statistic, rather than a shining example of God's love.[2]

For a woman to welcome your leadership as the woman did in 1:4, take loving leadership in your home. Becoming the chief servant in seeking to meet her and the children's spiritual, emotional, and physical needs won't alienate a godly woman—it will cause her to love you all the more. She will ask for your leadership. Especially as you add a fifth element of genuine love to your home.

5. AN INCREASING SECURITY IN THE RELATIONSHIP

So far, we've seen that Solomon's godly character has prompted many aspects of intimacy to grow and develop in his relationship with his fiancée. Yet, while his inner attitudes were the starting point for growth, his outward actions toward his bride-to-be were also key in developing their love. In particular, Solomon did something in their relationship that progressively moved his future bride from cold insecurity to security.

Listen to the words of a bride-to-be and see if you sense an element of insecurity in her statements:

I am black but lovely,
O daughters of Jerusalem . . . .
Do not stare at me because I am
  swarthy,
For the sun has burned me.
My mother's sons were angry
  with me;
They made me caretaker of the
  vineyards,
But I have not taken care of my
  own vineyard.   *(1:5–6)*

There is a sense in which all of us can feel insecure at times; but that is especially true in a relationship moving toward marriage. When we feel truly, unconditionally loved by another person, it can generate feelings of unworthiness and insecurity.

Often a young woman (or man) will question time and again, "Do you *really* love me?" "Am I really attractive to you?" "What about my background? My hair? My voice?"

These are the types of thoughts and feelings that the Shulammite woman experienced with Solomon in their love story. Here, she complains about something she fears might make her physically unattractive to the king. Unlike the "women of the court," who never ventured uncovered into the sun (and displayed milk-white skin as a result), she had been bronzed and burned in the fields. And while tanning salons may be popular with many women today, they wouldn't have lasted five minutes in Solomon's time, where suntanned skin was considered unattractive.

Not only that, she was a "working class" girl, in love and betrothed to a king! She had been made to work in her brothers' vineyards, doing common labor. As a result, she had little time to develop her own "vineyards" as well. Can you sense her insecurity?

Courtship and marriage are opportunities to either build security and deep acceptance into our loved ones' lives or to plant the seeds of insecurity and latter reap a harvest of distrust and distance.

Anne certainly had insecurities when Don proposed to her. He was from a wealthy family; she was a working class girl with a full-time job on top of her studies. He had time to work out at a local health club; with all her work and classes, she had neglected exercising and didn't feel that she looked her best.

Yet in the best of relationships, you'll see someone like the Shulammite woman or Anne move from increasing insecurity to a deeper security. And that's exactly what happened to both.

In the Song of Songs, we later read her words, "I am the rose of Sharon, the lily of the valleys" (2:1).

That's quite a contrast: from "Don't stare at me" to "I am the rose of Sharon" (the American Beauty rose of that day).

Genuine love breeds security in each season of life. You can see that clearly in how the Shulammite woman continues to picture their relationship.

Before the wedding, she says, "My beloved is mine, and I am his" (2:16). Notice the possessiveness there. It's the attitude, "He's mine! This one's taken!" That was during their courtship. Yet as time goes by and now that they're married, she shifts her words, "I am my beloved's and my beloved is mine" (6:3).

Though only a few words are rearranged, they reflect a deep internal change of attitude. Now it's not her hanging on to him. Rather, she's become so secure, she can say with confidence, "I am my beloved's." She is relaxing in his love. Then, even later in their relationship, she captures an ever increasing security level in the words, "I am my beloved's, and his desire is for me" (7:10).

This third time, she not only expresses the confidence she has in his love, but she's confident that "his desire is for me" alone. Now that's security!

For Anne, much the same thing happened. Don's love for her and her family was so consistent and real, it blew down her objections. On the day of their wedding, she stood before him, having gotten not only into great physical shape but feeling better about herself emotionally and spiritually than at any time in her life.

So it's time to ask the question: In your courtship or marriage, has the security level gone up each month you've been together, or down? Does your wife trust you more? Respect you more? Is she more confident around you and others than she used to be? Is her sense of her God-given worth higher today than it was a few years or even months ago?

Jayne came into her dating relationship with Ben with a strong relationship with Christ and a deep inner sense of worth. Now, two years later, she's emotionally tied to Ben, but suffering extreme spiritual and personal insecurities.

Why? He's a powerful, critical, perfectionist, who has made Jayne feel with each month that passes that she's less capable, less caring, and less adequate than when they first dated. Yet Ben gladly proposed to her, and plans are still being laid out for a wedding.

If you've been in a dating relationship for over a year and your sense of worth and security is much less than before you started dating, you can be fairly confident it's not genuine love you're in. At least not the type of biblical love that moves people to feel more adequate, more valuable, and more unconditionally accepted.

"But how do I develop an increasing security in my spouse's or fiancée's life?" Glad you asked, because that leads us to the sixth element of genuine love.

6. GIVING PRAISE

What caused such profound internal shifts of attitude and perception in Solomon's bride? One clear reason was found in a simple but powerful practice he mastered, the art of praise. Similarly, we build love and security by giving praise.

Over forty times in this small, eight-chapter book, Solomon puts his love into words with statements of praise. At times, reinforcing her beauty to him, and at other times encouraging her character and potential. It's the same thing that Don did with Anne, and Anne responded by "blooming" like a rose inside and out.

Notice in the first chapter on their courtship, Song 1, Solomon says to his bride, "To me, my darling, you are like my mare among the chariots of Pharaoh" (1:9).

"Wait a minute!" you might say. "Are you suggesting that when I meet my fiancée or wife for lunch today, I tell her, 'Honey, you look like a big horse . . . but you don't sweat as much'?"

Certainly not! Solomon isn't criticizing his bride here. He's using a powerful tool found throughout the Scriptures called an "emotional word picture" to praise her. When he really wants his words to hit home, he links his praise with an object or situation she is familiar with, and then provides her with a "picture" of his praise. Such a "one-two" punch of linking our words with a picture provides an image that is almost impossible to resist or forget.[3]

In Solomon's time, what made Egypt so powerful were the hundreds and hundreds of chariots their war machine possessed. These were the armored personnel carriers of their time. Yet the image Solomon compares his fiancée to is the single, white mare—chosen above all others —that alone pulled the Pharaoh's chariot.

To him, she was unique, outstanding among a thousand. And he communicated that specialness to her using a word picture of praise that she could not only hear but could "see" in her mind's eye.

But is praise really *that* important in building a strong relationship? Turn to their wedding night and you will see how Solomon's praise overcame his bride's insecurities there; it opened the door to a beautiful, intimate beginning to their marriage (Song 4).

None of us would like to have our wedding night recorded for all of history to view. It's a time for our first, deep physical intimacy; it's a glorious time, yet a private time. Yet that's exactly what is captured in the fourth chapter of this, God's blueprint for marital love.

The long procession and ceremony is now over and, alone at last, they move to the marriage bed. Yet before he touches her, Solomon will praise her seven times—each time using a different word picture. That number seven suggests completeness and perfection in the Bible, so his words of praise here seem worth noting. For example, he tells her,

> *How beautiful you are, my*
> *darling,*
> *How beautiful you are!*
> *Your eyes are like doves behind*
> *your veil.*   (4:1)

What's he saying with this picture? That she wears so much eye makeup that when she blinks her eyes, it's like a bird flapping its wings? No! In Old Testament times (and in the New Testament as well), the dove represented peace, and in New Testament times it represented peace and something—or actually *Someone*—else: the Holy Spirit. So when he looks at her eyes, he pictures the gentle, shy beauty he sees there as reflecting God's love. (And interestingly, in one of the few identical ways they praise each other, she will later praise him with the words, "His eyes are like doves" [5:12]).

Then he goes on to say,

> *Your hair is like a flock of goats*
> *That have descended from Mount*
>   *Gilead.*

Try telling your wife tonight that her hair looks like a goat and watch what happens! No touchy the toes, that's for sure!

Remember, a "word picture" is something that your hearer can identify with and is common in her experience. Unfortunately, most of us have neither been to Mount Gilead, nor even been around flocks of goats for any time.

In words his "shepherdess" bride will understand, he tells her that her hair is like the black, long-haired goats that are indigenous to Lebanon. He compares the goats that would come down a beautiful green hillside in the evening to black tresses of hair flowing from her head.

He praises her a third time, saying,

> *Your teeth are like a flock of newly shorn ewes*
> *Which have come up from their washing,*
> *All of which bear twins,*
> *And not one among them has lost her young.* (4:2)

What is his praise about now? Well, an obvious thing would be that he's happy she has all her teeth! None of them have been lost! But more than that, as a shepherdess, she would instantly recall the picture of the ewes after their shearing. Tossed into the water to clean them off, the female sheep come up sputtering and shaking to dry off, like overgrown puppies given a bath. Watching these freshly washed sheep, clean but shaking, the shepherdess's face brightens with a smile. That's when you see a person's teeth—in the midst of a smile.

Come on, Trent. Are you really saying that praising our financée or spouse—even using a word picture—will really build our relationships? Exactly. Because I've seen it work in my home and in the lives of hundreds of others as well.

One Valentine's Day when, despite my best intentions, I had to be out of town, a word picture helped my love life.

I had a speaking engagement, but I gave my wife, Cindy, a bouquet of flowers before I left and a big dinner at a special restaurant the night I got back. Still, I wasn't home for that important day, and as you can imagine, it wasn't the best option for either of us.

Before I left, I'd given her instructions to open a small envelope that held a message for her on Valentine's Day. Inside was a card that verbally expressed my love, and a common, everyday clothespin with a note attached. "Honey, you do such a great job of holding everything together when I have to go out of town," the note read. "I love you very much. John."

When I got home from my trip, guess what meant the most to my wife. Not the flowers. Not the dinner. It was something that was actually attached to our refrigerator! (What's really important to people often ends up on the icebox.) That clothespin I'd given her now had a magnet glued to the back, and a heart drawn on the front—and after several years, it still is on our refrigerator today.

I could have skipped the flowers and dinner and just given her the clothespin! Well, not exactly. However, I was shocked by how powerful that small picture of my love was, and how it went straight to her heart.

Are you a person who struggles with "praising" your wife? Does she really know, like Solomon's bride did, that she's unique, special, "one of a kind" as far as you're concerned?

If we want to build the type of love that is going to truly honor God and last over time, we need to be people who practice praise. And we need to be people who apply a seventh test to know whether we're practicing genuine love.

7. A FOCUS ON THE LOVED ONES

Out of sight, out of mind? That's not the biblical blueprint for genuinely being in love. Our thoughts are to ever drift to our loved ones. In Song 1:13–14 we read a seventh important guideline in recognizing or developing genuine love.

> *My beloved is to me a pouch of*
>   *myrrh*
> *Which lies all night between my*
>   *breasts.*
> *My beloved is to me a cluster of*
>   *henna blossoms*
> *In the vineyards of Engedi.*

Solomon's bride was picturing something common to ladies during Solomon's time. In a day and age without air-conditioning or bathing facilities like ours, perfume was much in use. And her word picture about their relationship is one of a sweet fragrance that stays with her all day and night.

Living in Phoenix, I enjoy those spring days each year when the orange trees blossom. Much of Phoenix is covered with orange trees, and for days most of the city is bathed in the most beautiful, sweet fragrance imaginable. (Forget the allergies those flowers cause for right now!)

Residents of this desert city can walk outside at high noon or midnight, and the smell is the same. That's how this bride-to-be pictures their love. Whether she wakes in the night or walks about during the day, her thoughts are of her beloved. She cannot escape the scent of myrrh around her, nor the fragrance of henna nearby; they are ever before her. In other words, for this woman, it's anything but "out of sight, out of mind." And that's how it should be for us men, in this seventh step to intimacy.

Joe was convinced that Amy was in love with him by her attitudes and actions. That is, until she went away on a summer mission trip. For three months she was out of the country. Joe wrote faithfully to his "girl," and even tried putting in two overseas calls; but after the first week, he never got a note from her.

Certainly her schedule was busy. Absolutely, she was involved in the important task of spreading the gospel. But when it came time for Joe to ask the hard questions, such as, "Are we really in love?" he couldn't check off this item from the list. And when Amy did get home, her attitude confirmed it. She hadn't thought of him, or at least not much. And it wasn't long before she was on to dating someone else.

Most married couples with children, jobs, and a thousand things fighting for their attention find it's difficult to focus much energy or thought on each other. I know couples who have never called each other from work to ask how the other's day was going; who can take trips lasting for days and never call home. I know men who can walk right into the home workshop or office after dinner without a second thought about what their wives might want to do that evening. In fact, in one recent week three couples visited my office for counseling with marital conflicts in these areas.

In courtship for sure, and in no small measure in a marriage, our thoughts and attention need to be disciplined to think on what we could do for our loved ones, how we can appreciate them, and how we can pray for them.

Our Lord commands us to take "every thought captive" (2 Corinthians 10:5) and to "think on the Lord" as part of our acknowledging Him each day. When Jesus wanted to discuss those who truly loved God, He said, "Where your treasure is, there will your heart be also" (Matthew 6:21). In other words, that person or object we "treasure" and place high value on, is where we'll spend our emotional energy.

When we truly value the Lord, our heart and emotions will make it natural for us to pray to Him, love Him, read His Word, and acknowledge His presence in our everyday lives. And the same thing is true when we reflect His love in loving our spouses. If you truly "treasure" your spouse, you'll have feelings for her! Emotionally you'll be drawn to your wife, appreciate her, think about her at times other than when she's in the car with you.

Ask yourself these questions: Do I truly "treasure" my spouse? Do I find in her the same high value that I did during our courtship? Most single men who are falling in love begin to think upon the woman of their lives more and more. Once a man is married, thoughts of his wife should be a regular part of his life.

If we never or rarely think of our wives outside of their physical presence, chances are their "value" to us is very low. We may say we love them, but one aspect of genuine love is demonstrated in the thoughts we have for them—something that comes naturally with someone we highly value.

Are you keeping a mental list of our steps to intimacy? If so, you're listing of what genuine, biblical love consists of looks similar to this:

1. Strong physical attraction exists.
2. The man displays a purified character.
3. Others see value in the one we love.
4. The man shows loving leadership, and the couple "runs together."
5. The lover seeks to move the one he loves from insecurity to increasing security.
6. Praise is commonplace and centered on the other's uniqueness.
7. The woman you love is in your thoughts and is a person whom you treasure.

There is a final step to intimacy. The eighth element of biblical love is first in terms of importance. See if you can pick it out in the word pictures below:

> "How beautiful you are, my
>   darling, how beautiful you are!
> Your eyes are like doves."

> "How handsome you are, my
>   beloved, and so pleasant!
> Indeed, our couch is luxuriant!
> The beams of our houses are
>   cedars,
> Our rafters, cypresses." (1:15–17)

Where have we seen those words, "Your eyes are like doves"? That's right! It was spoken on their wedding night, and in this book those words are spoken earlier by both the future bride and groom to picture their relationship. In other words, they saw things the same way, and each could look into the other's eyes and see a reflection of God's love—pictured in the dove.

8. A SPIRITUAL ONENESS

So as their courtship moves toward marriage, they're aligned spiritually. There's no oil and water here. No differing faiths, or one person in the relationship who loves God and reflects Him, while in the other's eyes is a cold disrespect or an "I couldn't care less" view of Christ.

If you're not seeing eye to eye *spiritually*, you don't have a secure foundation for marriage. We know that from the picture that follows.

"The beams of our houses are cedars, our rafters, cypresses" (1:17).

When the future bride looks in his eyes and then at the relationship that they are building together, she is assured that theirs is a spiritual relationship. How do we know this? In Old Testament times, cedars and cypress were primarily used in building the temple and tabernacle. Each pictured the finest of woods; and here, a strong, lasting structure is envisioned on which years of happiness could be built.

Sadly, such stability often is left out in marriages and not strongly considered in dating relationships. If you're not at the same place spiritually or if you're dating a person who doesn't know Christ, then you may have strong feelings for that person— but it isn't biblical love. When the storms of life, which *will* inevitably, crash down around your house, you won't have "cedars" and "cypresses" supporting it. You'll have a house of straw that the bad wolf of trials or temptation can blow down, and your relationship with it.

I realize those are strong words. But they come from someone who weekly tries through counseling to reassemble relationships that were never cemented in heaven to begin with. I'd rather hurt you now and head off "major league" hurt later.

We need God's love and spirit in our lives if we're to make a stand in these trying times. So don't expect God's blessing or power in a relationship where you are unequally yoked.

Does that mean if we're already married to an unbeliever that we can't have God's best? Certainly, we can individually grow deeply dependent on our Lord and see Him fill us with His strength and power to love our beloved unbeliever. We can find fulfillment *individually* and provide incredible love and support for our children. Yet the path to marital closeness won't be as easy, nor the foundation as strong, if both people can't look eye to eye and see Christ there.

If you're married to an unbeliever, redouble your prayers for her to come to know Christ. Not only is her eternity at stake, but the stakes are high that your marriage will not be all it could be as well.

If you're a Christian, but you're not at the place you'd like to be spiritually, then this would be a great time to recommit your life to Christ.

Right now, put down this booklet and ask Him to forgive you and set your feet back on His paths. Ask Him to guide you to the right resources, Scriptures, and a church that can help you build a structure for your home that is strong and secure.

As any construction worker will tell you, doing remodeling is harder work than building a new structure. But the Lord is able to help you clear away any shoddy materials you might have used in the past, and to replace it with planks of everlasting "cedars" and "cypresses" from His Word.

Eight steps to intimacy. Each one is part of building a loving, lasting relationship, a house of love. From physical attraction to a solid commitment to Christ, each can help develop love over a lifetime. But before we conclude with Solomon's summary about genuine love, let me leave you with one final word picture.

Just before their wedding, Solomon's bride gives her soon-to-be-husband some God-inspired advice. It's the same advice I'll leave with you as well. As she looks at their relationship, she says,

> *Catch the foxes for us,*
> *The little foxes that are ruining*
> * the vineyards,*
> *While our vineyards are in*
> * blossom.*   (2:15)

Every relationship has those "little" problems that can eat away at our emotional and spiritual vitality. Perhaps it's our tone of voice that communicates anger and harshness. It may be our uncontrolled spending that is eating away at our spouse's trust level. Or maybe it's our lack of taking spiritual leadership as we stay home to watch the football game instead of getting up and going to church (and maybe making a video recording of the game to watch later).

I'm not sure what the "foxes" are in your relationship. But I do know that they can quickly become lions that men and women can't avoid facing.

If you've located five or more of these keys to intimacy in your own love relationship, then good for you. No doubt love is growing in your marriage or dating relationship. You may still have some "foxes" to catch, but you're well on your way to a God-honoring relationship. But if you are down below five, you may have some lions just waiting to spring out of the closet, ready to attack your marriage.

What can you do to chase those lions? Here are some suggestions. Get in a small support group. Attend a Christian marriage or family conference.[4] Pick up an inspirational book on your relationship with God and your marriage or courtship by Chuck Swindoll, James Dobson, Max Lucado, or Ken Gire. Become a regular attender of a church that preaches and teaches God's Word regularly. Be willing to receive Christian counseling if you need to, recognizing like Solomon that "only fools despise wisdom and correction" (Proverbs 1:7).

As you evaluate your courtship and marriage against God's clear picture of love, may you learn to love Christ more and your spouse or friend better. Basing our love on His Word will not only enrich our lives beyond our expectations or hopes, but will provide the church with the greatest evangelistic tool it could have—distinctively Christian homes.

NOTES

1. For a further discussion on reasons men don't lead and how they can become great leaders in their home, see *The Hidden Value of a Man*, by Gary Smalley and John Trent.

2. *Powerful Personalities*, by Tim Kimmel, has an excellent discussion of controllers and how to overcome this tendency.

3. The concept of emotional word pictures is explored fully in *The Language of Love*, by Gary Smalley and John Trent.

4. Announcements of Christian marriage conferences often appear in church bulletins and community newspapers. One conference I enjoy leading is "The Blessing," which describes how to have healthy relationships among family members. For information about attending this conference, write me at Encouraging Words, 12629 N. Tatum Blvd., Suite 420, Phoenix, AZ 85032.

John Trent has expanded these
powerful thoughts on intimacy in
*Love for All Seasons:
Eight Ways to Nurture Intimacy*.
This insightful new book includes
more vivid stories,
thought-provoking questions,
and even a personal or
small group study guide.
An audio version of the book
is available as well.

Contact your local bookstore
for more information.